PRAYERS FOR MOTHERS AND CHILDREN

First English edition 1943
Second edition, enlarged 1968
Third edition, enlarged 1983

The lecture is translated from shorthand reports unrevised by the lecturer. The original German title is *Gebete für Mütter und Kinder* and contains the lecture entitled: *Das Leben zwischen der Geburt und dem Tode als Spiegelung des Lebens zwischen Tod und neuer Geburt*. This English edition is published in agreement with the Rudolf Steiner Nachlassverwaltung, Dornach, Switzerland.

© Rudolf Steiner Press, London.

British Library Cataloguing in Publication Data

Steiner, Rudolf
    Prayers for mothers and children.
    1. Mothers—Prayer-books and devotions
    2. Anthroposophy
    I. Title
    299'.935   BP596.P7
    ISBN 0–85440–195–4

Printed and bound in Great Britain at
The Camelot Press Ltd, Southampton

RUDOLF STEINER

PRAYERS
FOR MOTHERS
AND CHILDREN

Translated from the German by Eileen V. Hersey

With a single lecture, Dornach
2nd February 1915, translated from the
German by Christian von Arnim:

Life between Birth and Death
as a mirror of life
between Death and a new Birth

RUDOLF STEINER PRESS
LONDON

CONTENTS

RUDOLF STEINER

PRAYERS

FOR MOTHERS

AND CHILDREN

Translated from the German by Eileen V. Hersey

With a single lecture, Dornach
2nd February 1915, translated from the
German by Christian von Arnim:

Life between Birth and Death
as a mirror of life
between Death and a new Birth

RUDOLF STEINER PRESS
LONDON

CONTENTS

RUDOLF STEINER

PRAYERS

FOR MOTHERS

AND CHILDREN

Translated from the German by Eileen V. Hersey

With a single lecture, Dornach
2nd February 1915, translated from the
German by Christian von Arnim:

Life between Birth and Death
as a mirror of life
between Death and a new Birth

RUDOLF STEINER PRESS
LONDON

CONTENTS

Ich schau in die Sternenwelt –
Ich verstehe der Sterne Glanz,
Wenn ich in ihm schauen Kann
Gottes weisheitvolles Weltenlenken
Ich schau' in's eigne Herz –
Ich verstehe des Herzens Schlag,
Wenn ich in ihm spüren Kann
Gottes gütevolles Menschenlenken.
Ich verstehe nichts vom Sternenglanz
Und auch nichts vom Herzensschlag
Wenn ich Gott nicht schau' und spüre
Und Gott hat meine Seele
Geführt in dieses Leben;
Er wird sie führen zu immer neuem Leben
So sagt, wer richtig denken Kann.
Und jedes Jahr, das man weiter lebt
Spricht mehr von Gott und Seelenewigkeit.

Facsimile of Rudolf Steiner's prayer
"Ich schau' in die Sternenwelt —"
(see pages 58 and 59)

THE PUBLICATION OF LECTURES HELD
BY RUDOLF STEINER

The foundation of anthroposophically orientated spiritual science is laid in the works which were written and published by Rudolf Steiner (1861-1925). At the same time Steiner held numerous lectures and courses both for the general public and for Members of the Theosophical (later Anthroposophical) Society in the years between 1900 and 1924. It was not his original wish to have these lectures published which were without exception of a spontaneous nature and conceived as "oral communications not intended for print." However, after an increasing number of incomplete and erroneous listeners' transcripts had been printed and circulated, he found it necessary to have the notes regulated. He entrusted this task to Marie Steiner von Sivers. She was made responsible for the choice of stenographers, the supervision of their transcripts and the necessary revision of texts before publication. As Rudolf Steiner was only in a very few instances able to correct the notes himself his reservation in respect to all publications of his lectures must be taken into account: "Errors occurring in transcripts which I myself have been unable to revise will just have to be tolerated."

In Chapter 35 of his autobiography, Rudolf Steiner expounds on the relationship between his lectures for Members which were initially only circulated internally and his public writings. The relevant text is printed at the end of this volume. What is expressed there also applies to the lecture courses directed towards a restricted audience already familiar with the principles of spiritual science.

After Marie Steiner's death (1867-1948) the editing of a "Complete Works of Rudolf Steiner" was commenced according to her directions. The volume at hand constitutes a part of this complete edition.

LIFE BETWEEN BIRTH AND DEATH
AS A MIRROR OF LIFE
BETWEEN DEATH AND A NEW BIRTH

The opportunity has often arisen in our discussions to point out that those who really want to understand life and existence would be wrong to proceed from the premise that life and existence are simple. Attention has often had to be drawn to the complexity and the manifold nature of cosmic harmony, of which the human being is an integral part, even if only for the reason that one continuously hears people say that truth — and normally they mean truth concerning the highest things — has to be simple. People like it best if someone tells them that this truth about the highest things does not really need to be studied, but that one simply possesses it without any work — just like that.

Everyone — and I have said this before — is willing to admit that they cannot understand the workings of a watch if they have not learnt how the interaction of the cogs and the rest of the mechanism functions. Only as far as the great, magnificent and mighty workings of the cosmos is concerned do people wish comprehension without effort. The basic aim of spiritual science, however, is to permit us slowly and gradually to reach a real understanding of the sense, the meaning of existence and life.

Today I want to add something to the things with which we have already dealt, proceeding from concepts and ideas which are already familiar to us, ideas with which we have often concerned ourselves. To begin with, it has to be said from the spiritual scientific point of view: outer existence which we inhabit is maya, the great illusion. But I have emphasised that within a western world conception it cannot

1

be our view that everything which surrounds us is illusion in the sense that it is unreal. Not the world as such which affects our senses, which we grasp with our reason, is maya; in its innermost being this world is true reality. But the way that the human being perceives it, the way it appears to the human being, turns the world into maya, turns it into a great illusion. And when we reach a stage through the inward work of the soul where we find the deeper foundation of the things revealed to the senses and of the things stated by reason, we will soon recognise the extent to which the outer world is an illusion. Because it appears in its true light, as it really is, when we know how to supplement and permeate it with those things which must remain hidden in our initial observation of the world.

It is precisely the thing which gives the human being his status, gives him his dignity and purpose, that the cosmos does not treat him like an immature child to whom truth is presented on a platter, but that it is taken for granted that he acquires truth through his own work, his life's work. In a certain sense the cosmic powers count on our help in gaining truth, they count on our freedom and dignity.

Now the whole of human life as it initially progresses between birth and death is maya, an illusion. It has to be an illusion because when we view the world only as outward physical objects and events we ignore the other aspect of the world and of existence in so far as it affects the human being, we ignore the things which the human being experiences between death and a new birth.

One might well say that one can understand human life between birth and death simply by observing it. Why is the other side, the life between death and a new birth necessary? But this already is a false conception for the simple reason that the life between birth and death is a reflection of the life between death and a new birth. The things which we experience in the life preceding our present physical life are reflected in the life between birth and death.

In order to understand this reflection, it is necessary to consider two further things. The first is that we observe certain stages, certain highlights in our life between birth and death and investigate how these are reflections of the life between death and a new birth. Then it is necessary to realise that the life between death and a new birth is connected to a much greater extent with the unknown worlds of which we speak in spiritual science: the events which occurred on what we call the old saturn, the old sun and the old moon before the development of our earth. These events on saturn, sun and moon are connected much more strongly with our existence between death and a new birth than with the life between birth and death.

We might even say that the life between death and birth is influenced everywhere and from all sides by those past lives which we know as the past planetary lives of saturn, sun and moon. The effect of the latter on our hidden earth-life between death and a new birth is in turn reflected in the life between birth and death. Thus the life between birth and death is a reflection of the events which occur between death and a new birth which are in turn influenced by events on old saturn, old sun and old moon.

Certain highpoints, certain stages of our earth-life must be observed more closely for a better understanding of this process.

The first event of earthly life is what in human physical existence we call conception, followed by the embryonic stage. Only then does the birth of the human being, his entry on to the physical plane, occur.

Now a peculiar circumstance is revealed to spiritual science. There is only one event in the whole of human life, in so far as it is spent in a physical body, which is solely connected with the earth, which is in a sense explicable purely from earth-existence. That event is conception. Nothing in human life other than conception is fundamentally connected with earth-existence immediately and exclusively. I must emphasise the word "exclusively". Conception has no connection with the life of moon, sun and saturn; the causes of the event which occurs with conception originate in earth-life.

Because external biology, external science, is concerned in the main only with physical existence, and from its point of view considers everything related to the life of the moon, sun and saturn as folly, this external science can discover the truth in the physical sense of the word only about conception. That is why we find, when we read works such as Ernst Haeckel, that they emphasise those aspects which relate the human being with processes in other organisms, and that those things are dealt with which are in some way connected with conception. An examination of external science in this respect will find this to be true. Physical external science, when it investigates the processes in the human being, usually descends to the level of the most simple cells. Such cells, forms from which the human being, too, originates (he develops from the fertilised egg), did not exist on old saturn, old sun and old moon. They are to be found only on earth, and on earth the joining of cells takes place which is considered of such importance by external science.

This particular stage of our life is nothing but the reflection of a real event which takes place before conception already and which is connected with human life. In the last period of our life between death and a new birth, but also at the time of physical conception, we are clearly in the spiritual world. Something is continually happening to us on a spiritual level, and conception is nothing but a reflection, maya, of this happening. But the event which takes place in the spiritual world is one which occurs between sun and earth in such a manner that the female element is influenced by the sun and the male element is influenced by the earth. Thus the event of conception mirrors the interaction between sun and earth.

This event, which human beings frequently reduce to a level degrading for mankind, therefore becomes the most significant of mysteries, the reflection of a cosmic event. It

4

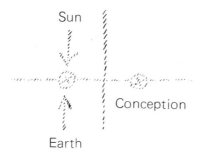

Sun

Conception

Earth

is of interest to draw attention to some details here. When a person approaches the time of his renewed entry to earth, a soul-like image of the parents through whom he will enter the earth is formed. How he comes to choose one particular set of parents we can discuss at another time; this is connected with karma. But the thing to which I want to draw attention today is that the person progressing towards birth receives an image of the physical world initially mainly through the mother, he primarily sees the mother. He receives an image of the father — and I would ask you to consider this because it is important — because the mother carries an image of the father in her soul. Thus the father is seen through the image which the mother carries in her soul.

This is, of course, expressed in somewhat simplified form, but it is essentially correct. These supersensible processes can only be expressed by giving their essential character. In order that you do not receive too fixed an image, I want to add that, for example, if it is important that the soul and spiritual inheritance from the father's side plays a special role, if special soul and spiritual characteristics of the father are to be passed on to the human being approaching birth, a direct image of the father can also be created. But the image of the mother weakens to the degree that the image of the father is directly observed.

The next step of physical existence on earth is the life between conception and birth. This stage, too, — we call it the embryonic stage — reflects an event which takes place in the spiritual world before the process mentioned earlier. Whilst birth in physical life obviously follows conception, that of which birth is a reflection precedes the sun-earth process which is mirrored in conception.

The existence of the human being between conception and birth can certainly not be explained from the circumstances prevalent upon earth, and to try and explain it on the basis of physical forces and laws is pure nonsense, because it is the reflection of a process before birth which is essentially influenced by the remains of the sun and the moon from an earlier stage than the earth. It is a process which takes place between the sun and the moon, and thus is in essence a spiritual one.

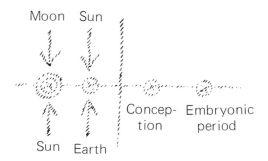

The forces which are active here are primarily those in play between the sun and moon. Outer science has still preserved an awareness of this fact by calculating the embryonic period in lunar months, saying that it occurs over ten lunar months.

In this sense we have to take into account that in our life between death and a new birth we are subject to a real influence from the sun and moon, but that in our following physical life we reflect this process, which is a sun and moon process, between conception and birth.

It should be noted that the expression "reflect" is used here in a somewhat different sense from the physical one. In physical reflection the object and the image are simultaneously present, but here we have the real process taking place before birth. The reflection occurs later in time. It is thus maya of a spiritual process before birth.

The next thing to take into account is the period between birth and that frequently mentioned, important time in human life when we start to unfold our ego-consciousness, when we consciously start to call ourselves "I". This can be called the real period of childhood. The period of first childhood — we can also call it the period of infanthood — is again the reflection of a process which lies even further in the spiritual past. The real process which is mirrored in the period when we start to babble without establishing the link between speech and ego-consciousness, is a reflection of a process from before birth which extends even further into the cosmos. Here there is interaction between the sun and all the planets which belong to the sun, that is, the sun and its encircling planets with the exception of the moon. The forces which are at play between the sun and its planets affect our life between death and a new birth, and what is created thereby long before our birth is reflected in the life of early childhood.

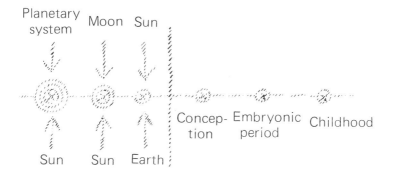

7

One can see from this that the child's life is affected by the reflections of things which are even further removed from physical existence than the moon. This has a deeply important practical result; it has the result that the human being must not be diverted in this period of his life from the forces which he receives and the assimilation of the forces which he has already received, respectively. Consider the situation. Before our birth, forces from the cosmos at play between the sun and its planets affect us. These forces are present in the child which has passed through birth and has entered earth-life. These forces want to emerge from the child. They really are in the child. In this sense the child with its innermost being is a messenger from heaven, and these forces want to emerge. Fundamentally we can do nothing more than allow these forces the greatest possible opportunity to appear. That is basically all that we must attempt educationally in the infant-stage of the human being: we must not disturb the forces which are trying to emerge.

Such a view brings about a humble attitude. Whilst man normally believes that he can represent much to the child, it is necessary above all that the forces which want to emerge are diverted as little as possible. Not that the educating human being means nothing to the child; he does, because what emerges is a reflection which must be made real by the educator, which must be substantiated.

Our task as educators can be shown in the following way: if we have a reflected object we have to fill the image with something which gives it more inward strength than it has purely as an image. Man is indeed born as a reflection and he has to gain the strength to make the image real. That, precisely, is his development between birth and death.

The reflections of the processes which we gained from the cosmos before birth want to emerge and must be diverted as little as possible. Through our influence we have to make them into reality, and in so far as we can make them into a false reality — that is, try to make corrections — we can

8

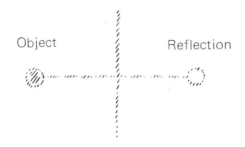

Object   Reflection

divert them. But they are something spiritual.

Now you can understand the greatly significant consequence which results from this. The person who brings up a child is called upon to have in his own soul, which has its concurrent existence with the child, supersensible ideas and feelings. For all purely material ideas and feelings which are made accessible to the child interfere with its development.

The question is often asked: how can we best bring up a child? As with so many things, it is not a matter of setting up a few principles which we can carry around with us and which determine our actions. It is important that we start with ourselves, that we make an effort to carry within us a fund of supersensible ideas, that we are permeated by an attitude and by feelings which enter the supersensible. For these have a far greater effect than what we can achieve by outer intellectual principles, by intellectual pedagogy. A loving mind which is permeated by the supersensible world and thus deepens all feelings, thereby creates a situation of introducing a certain — and please do not misunderstand this word — religiosity into the upbringing of the child, which consists of loving a being sent from the spiritual world; which consists of raising our love of the child into a spiritual sphere with the feeling that in extending our hands to the child we are giving the child something as representatives of those forces which are not to be found on earth but in the supersensible.

All the things which can be worked out concerning pedagogical principles will bear little fruit as long as this science proceeds along materialistic lines. Only the things which are the result of spiritual science will bear fruit for the true education of the child. And the most important thing is how we develop ourselves. In the outer, material world we may achieve much by what we do. As educators we achieve much more by what we are. This should be well noted and could well serve as a motto for good education.

Then comes the age of boyhood and girlhood, an age when we are still being educated, but in a different way than in the period of infancy. That is the next stage to be considered. It includes the whole period from the time when the human being consciously starts to call himself "I" up to the point when he is released from education as such, when he freely enters life, the time when as a well or badly educated person he has to make his own way in the whirlpool of life.

This, too, is a reflection, outwardly maya, of previous events. The realities again lie between death and a new birth. Here the whole planetary system from the sun to saturn — or neptune, according to most recent astronomy — is at work. The whole of the planetary system works together with the stars in the heavens, and what occurs between the stars and the whole planetary system are the forces which are alive in us during the time of our education.

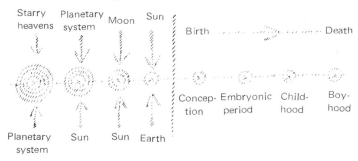

So little of the reality of the human being can be explained purely from processes on earth that the only way to understand

him in the period of his schooling is if there is a clear understanding that forces are at play in him in the totality of his
life which are not on earth, which are not even in the planetary
system, but which lie and are at work outside the planetary
sphere in harmony with the stars.

When we are faced with a child which can already call
itself "I", which we approach, therefore, in a certain sense as
human being, we must be quite clear that something lives in
him which is the reflection of something which is active not
only outside our earth, but outside our planetary system.

That is why the things which have been said about the
early education of the child are true in far greater measure
for the following periods of education; namely the statement:
good pedagogy will only come into existence when it is
drawn from spiritual science, when the teacher is aware that
outside the planetary system a world exists which unfolds in
the human being, when it is more than theoretical knowledge
in him and permeates his feelings and attitudes, when he
himself has experienced the truth of this world beyond the
planets. The unsure steps of such a teacher are often better
than the ingenious pedagogical principles of a materialistic
teacher. Because the insecure steps, our actions undertaken
in ignorance, improve in the course of our life. But the things
which occur because of what we are do not correct themselves in the course of our life.

It is to be wished that among the things which spiritual
science must metamorphose or transform is also the following:
it should be increasingly understood that those who want to
become teachers and educators — that includes fundamentally
also all those who want to become parents — should ensure
that they become good educators by the assimilation of
spiritual ideas gathered in their soul. In order to become a
good educator, the bulk of the work has to be undertaken on
oneself. And it is more important as regards a teacher, for
example, that he lives wholeheartedly in the material to be
dealt with in school the next day, before he enters the school,

11

than that he has the best possible pedagogical principles on how to do this or that. After he has grown to love the subject, grown to love it inwardly in the spirit, he can even stumble in the lesson — although I do not want to recommend that — and he will do a better job than the person who enters school with all sorts of principles strait-jacketed into his brain and who knows everything about the most correct way to set about things.

We know that at present in the world things still take place the other way round. Those who are to be educators today are tested above all for the things which they know, for the content of the knowledge they have assimilated. It is almost true to say that they are tested on the things which they can find in books, on which they can establish a library. The things which can be looked up in a library, if one has been taught how to do so, are the things which are largely examined. In teachers' examinations the important things ought not to be what the person concerned can easily find if he needs it; knowledge ought not to be the important things, but each teacher ought to be examined instead how in his attitudes, his feelings, he can establish a link with knowledge of, with feeling for the development of the whole universe capable of being won by human beings. The attitude towards human and cosmic development ought to be the yardstick for whether someone is a good teacher or not. Then, of course, those would fail the examinations who only knew the most material and those would pass the examinations with best results who were good human beings in the spiritual sense.

In the end that will also come about. The direction in which we must move in the end is the following: a human being who is not good, whose soul does not incline towards the spiritual life, would fail the teachers' examination in future, however much he knew, even if he had everything at his fingertips which is required as knowledge today.

Thus the field will develop here which places emphasis less on intellectual knowledge than on the development of the whole of the soul. Let it be emphasised once more: the important thing is not that we are of value by our influence in the outer material field, by what we do. As educators we are above all of value by what we are.

It is important that we take account of everything which relates to that real process reflected in conception. All that belongs to the earth. But in so far as it lies before birth it belongs to the interaction of sun and earth, it takes place in the earth's aura. A significant spiritual event takes place in the earth's aura before human conception which is reflected in conception. What takes place between conception and birth is in reality interaction between sun and moon, and this is essentially a repeat of events which took place earlier during the old moon period of the earth.

In the embryonic period a real event is reflected which is like a repeat of the event which took place on the old moon. Similarly the process which occurs between the end of childhood, the point when the human being consciously calls himself "I", and birth is a repeat of the influence of the old sun. The things which occur even before that, which are reflected in the period of education, are a repeat of the old saturn stage of the earth.

And then, when our education is finished and we enter the world well or badly educated, what events are reflected there? Then the events are mirrored which lie even before the saturn period, which are not part of the visible world at all to such an extent that they do not even have a correlation in the outward stars. One can say of the correlations of our experiences up to the end of our education that they are still visible. The outermost stars which are still visible still bear a relationship to it. But our subsequent experience, our subsequent development belongs to the invisible world. We are released from the visible cosmos when we have truly completed our education.

And then, of course, it is a matter of enriching, or having already enriched, our soul with the truths of the supersensible worlds. That is the only way to find the true path through life. Otherwise we are puppets, guided by forces which are not meant to do so. The person who freely enters the world after the reflection of the saturn stage in his development and has no idea in his soul of a spiritual world, is not in the element of his vocation but is carried along by invisible forces as the puppet is carried along by the forces contained in the strings which are pulled.

To assimilate what spiritual science can give means becoming a human being; means not remaining a puppet of the sense world, but reaching freedom which is the element, so to speak, in which the human being lives and works during his life. Indeed, freedom can only be understood in those terms which do not originate in the sense world. For everything that is given us from the sense world cannot make us free. This I had in mind when I wrote my *Philosophy of Freedom*,* where I emphasised how — even without reference to the ideas of spiritual science, as it were — the foundations of ethics, of morals have to be described as moral imagination; that is to say, they have to be discovered on the basis of moral imagination, on the basis of something that is not contained in any sense world, although of course morals should not be considered as being pure phantasy. The whole chapter written on moral imagination is an affirmation that the human being throughout his life, in so far as he wants to spend it in freedom, has to recognise his connection with something which is not a reflection of the sense world but which has to arise freely in him, which he carries within himself, which is more majestic than the visible stars, which cannot be gained from the sense world but only through an inward, creative process. That is the meaning of the chapter on moral imagination.

These thoughts were again intended to show the numerous relations of which we are a part in life. As the life before

*Published by Rudolf Steiner Press, London, 1979.

14

birth is preparatory for its reflection, so the reflection between birth and death is in turn preparatory for the spiritual life which follows between death and a new birth. The more we can take from this life into the life between death and a new birth, the richer the development of that life will be. Even the concepts which we have to learn concerning that life, concerning the truths between death and a new birth, these concepts have to be different to those which we have to learn from physical maya, if we want to understand it. Some of those concepts which have to be learnt for an understanding of the other aspect of human life, passing between death and a new birth, can be found in the Vienna lecture cycle of 1914, "The Inner Nature of Man and life between death and a new birth". It is sometimes quite difficult to expose step by step the concepts and ideas which are required for the different nature of this life. And you will notice particularly in reading such a lecture cycle the struggle to find expressions which somewhat reflect these quite different conditions.

At this time in particular, when the deaths of dear members have occurred in our anthroposophical life, I want to draw attention to one point. The occurrence of death plays a different role in the life between death and a new birth than does the point of birth in our current life between birth and death. The time of birth is not usually remembered by the human being under normal circumstances of physical life. But the time of death is one which leaves a most deep impression for the whole life between death and a new birth; it is remembered most of all, it is always present, as it were, but in a different form than as seen from this side of life. From this side of life death appears as a disintegration, something of which man has fear and dread. From the other side, death appears as the luminous beginning of spiritual experience, as something which spreads sun-like over the whole life between death and a new birth, which warms the soul with joy and which is repeatedly looked back on with deep understanding. That is the moment of death. To express it in earthly terms: the most joyful, the most rapturous thing between death and a new birth is the point of death when it is experienced from that side.

If from a materialistic point of view we have formed the idea that the human being loses consciousness with death, if we have no real conception of the way consciousness develops, and I say this particularly today because we are thinking of dear ones who have died recently, if we find great difficulty in imagining the existence of a consciousness beyond death, if we believe that consciousness fades, and it seems to appear that consciousness fades with death, then we have to be clear: it is not true. For consciousness is exceedingly lucid, and only because the human being is unused in the initial period after death to living in this extremely clear consciousness does something similar to the state of sleep occur initially immediately after death.

But this state of sleep is the opposite of the one which we spend in ordinary life. In ordinary life we sleep because the level of consciousness is reduced. After death we are unconscious in a certain sense because consciousness is too strong, too overwhelming, because we live completely in the consciousness and the requirement in the initial days is to accustom ourselves to this heightened state of consciousness. When we then succeed in orientating ourselves sufficiently that we feel the emergence from the wealth of world thoughts: that was you! — in the moment when we learn to distinguish our past earth-life from the wealth of world thoughts, we experience in this wealth of consciousness the moment of which it can be said: we awaken. We might be awakened by an event which was particularly significant in our life and which is also of significance for events after our earth-life.

Thus it is a matter of growing accustomed to supersensible consciousness, to consciousness which is not built on the foundations and supports of the physical world, but which is sufficient in itself. That is what we call "awakening" after death. One could describe this awakening as a probing by the will which, as you know and also can see from the above-mentioned lecture cycle, is able to develop particularly after death. I spoke there of a feeling-like will and a will-like feeling. When this will-like feeling starts to venture into the supersensible world, when it makes the first probe, then it starts to awaken.

Those are things which, circumstances permitting, we will discuss further.

PRAYERS FOR MOTHERS AND CHILDREN

Licht und Wärme
Des göttlichen Weltengeistes
Hülle mich ein.

May light and warmth
From the divine Spirit of the Cosmos
Enfold me.

Gesprochen von der Mutter

VOR DER GEBURT

Und des Kindes Seele,
Sie sei mir gegeben
Nach Eurem Willen
Aus den geistigen Welten.

NACH DER GEBURT

Und des Kindes Seele,
Sie sei von mir geleitet
Nach Eurem Willen
In die geistigen Welten.

Spoken by the Mother

BEFORE BIRTH

And the child's soul
Be given to me
According to your will
From spirit worlds.

AFTER BIRTH

And the child's soul
Be guided by me
According to your will
Into spirit worlds.

GEBET FÜR GANZ KLEINE KINDER
gesprochen von einem Erwachsenen

In dich ströme Licht, das dich ergreifen kann.
Ich begleite seine Strahlen mit meiner Liebe Wärme.
Ich denke mit meines Denkens besten Frohgedanken
An deines Herzens Regungen.
Sie sollen dich stärken,
Sie sollen dich tragen,
Sie sollen dich klären.
Ich möchte sammeln vor deinen Lebensschritten
Meine Frohgedanken,
Dass sie sich verbinden deinem Lebenswillen
Und er in Stärke sich finde
In aller Welt,
Immer mehr,
Durch sich selbst.

PRAYER FOR VERY SMALL CHILDREN
spoken by an adult

May light stream into you that can take hold of you.
I follow its rays with the warmth of my love.
I think with my thinking's best thoughts of joy
On the stirrings of your heart.
May they strengthen you,
May they carry you,
May they cleanse you.
I want to gather my thoughts of joy
Before the steps of your life,
That they unite with your will for life,
So that it finds itself with strength
In the world,
Ever more,
Through itself.

GEBET FÜR KLEINE KINDER, DIE SCHON SELBST BETEN

Vom Kopf bis zum Fuss
Bin ich Gottes Bild,
Vom Herzen bis in die Hände
Fühl ich Gottes Hauch.
Sprech ich mit dem Mund,
Folg ich Gottes Willen.
Wenn ich Gott erblick'
Überall, in Mutter, Vater,
In allen lieben Menschen,
In Tier und Blume,
In Baum und Stein,
Gibt Furcht mir nichts,
Nur Liebe zu allem,
Was um mich ist.

PRAYER FOR LITTLE CHILDREN
WHO THEMSELVES ALREADY PRAY *

From my head to my feet
I am the image of God.
From my heart to my hands
I feel the breath of God.
When I speak with my mouth
I follow God's will.
When I behold God
Everywhere, in mother, father,
In all dear people,
In beast and flower,
In tree and stone,
Nothing brings fear,
But love to all
That is around me.

* Not to be taught specially. An adult says it every evening; the child gradually repeats individual words, then lines, and so learns the whole prayer.

Seh ich die Sonne,
Denk ich Gottes Geist.
Rühr ich die Hand,
Lebt in mir Gottes Seele.
Mach ich einen Schritt,
Wandelt in mir Gottes Wille.
Und wenn einen Menschen ich sehe,
Lebt Gottes Seele in ihm.
Und so lebt sie auch
In Tier und Pflanze und Stein.
Nimmer Furcht kann mich erreichen,
Wenn ich denke Gottes Geist,
Wenn ich lebe Gottes Seele,
Wenn ich wandle in Gottes Willen.

When I see the sun,
I think God's spirit.
When I use my hand,
God's soul lives in me.
When I take a step,
God's will walks in me.
And when I see other people,
God's soul lives in them.
And so it lives, too,
In beast and plant and stone.
Fear can never reach me
When I think God's spirit,
When I live God's soul,
When I walk in God's will.

In one manuscript the word "thank" takes the place of "think" in the second
and twelfth lines.

Um mich leben viele Wesen,
Um mich sind viele Dinge,
In meinem Herzen auch —
Spricht Gott zur Welt.
Und spricht am besten,
Wenn ich lieben kann
Alle Wesen, alle Menschen.

Es leben die Pflanzen
In Sonnenlichtes Kraft.
Es wirken die Menschenleiber
In Seelenlichtes Macht.
Und was der Pflanze
Der Sonne Himmelslicht,
Das ist dem Menschenleibe
Das Geistes-Seelenlicht.

Round me many beings live,
Round me there are many things,
Also in my heart —
God speaks to the world.
And he speaks best,
When I can love,
Everything and everyone.

The plants are alive
In the sunlight's strength.
Human bodies are at work
In the soul-light's power.
What the sunlight of heaven
Is to the plant,
So to man's body
Is the spirit's soul-light.

MORGENGEBET

Sonne, du leuchtest über meinem Haupte,
Sterne, ihr scheinet über Feld und Stadt,
Tiere, ihr reget und beweget euch auf der Erdenmutter,
Pflanzen, ihr lebet durch die Erd- und Sonnenkraft.
Steine, ihr festigt Tier und Pflanze
Und mich, den Menschen,
Dem des Gottes Macht
Lebt in Kopf und Herz,
Der mit Gottes Kraft
Durchwandelt die Welt.

MORNING PRAYER

Sun, you cast your light above my head,
Stars, you shine over field and town,
Beasts, you stir and move on Mother Earth,
Plants, you live by strength of Earth and Sun,
Stones, you give firmness to beast and plant
And to me, the human being,
In whose head and heart
Lives the power of God,
And who walks through the world
With the strength of God.

ABENDGEBET

Mein Herz dankt,
Dass mein Auge sehen darf,
Dass mein Ohr hören darf,
Dass ich wachend fühlen darf
In Mutter und Vater,
In allen lieben Menschen,
In Sternen und Wolken:
Gottes Licht,
Gottes Liebe,
Gottes Sein,
Die mich schlafend
Leuchtend
Liebend
Gnadespendend schützen.

EVENING PRAYER

My heart gives thanks
That my eye may see,
That my ear may hear,
That, waking, I may feel
In mother and father,
In all dear people,
In stars and clouds:
The Light of God,
The Love of God,
The Being of God,
Which, when I sleep,
Shining,
Loving,
Bestowing grace,
Protect me.

Der Sonne Licht
Es hellt den Tag
Nach finstrer Nacht:
Der Seele Kraft,
Sie ist erwacht
Aus Schlafes Ruh':
Du meine Seele,
Sei dankbar dem Licht,
Es leuchtet in ihm
Des Gottes Macht;
Du meine Seele,
Sei tüchtig zur Tat.

The light of the sun,
It brightens the day
When dark night is past:
The strength of the soul,
It has woken up
From restful sleep:
You, oh my soul,
Give thanks to the light,
For in it there shines
The power of God;
You, oh my soul,
Be active in deeds.

Es keimen die Pflanzen
Im Erdengrund,
Es zieht die Sonne
Aus Finsternis
Sie in das Licht:
So keimet das Gute
Im Menschenherzen.
Es ziehet die Seele
Aus Geistesgründen —
Die Kraft des Ich.

The plant seeds quicken
In the ground of the earth,
The sun draws them up
From darkness
To light:
So quickens the Good
In human hearts.
The soul draws out
From spirit grounds —
The strength of the Self.

TISCHGEBET

Es keimen die Pflanzen in der Erdennacht,
Es sprossen die Kräuter durch der Luft Gewalt,
Es reifen die Früchte durch der Sonne Macht.

So keimet die Seele in des Herzens Schrein,
So sprosset des Geistes Macht im Licht der Welt,
So reifet des Menschen Kraft in Gottes Schein.

GRACE AT MEALTIMES *

In the darkness of earth the seeds are awakened,
In the power of the air the plants are quickened,
In the might of the sun the fruits are ripened.

In the shrine of the heart the soul is awakened,
In the light of the world the spirit is quickened,
In the glory of God man's powers are ripened.

* Rendering by A. C. Harwood

Es keimen die Wurzeln in der Erde Nacht,
Es sprossen die Blätter durch der Luft Gewalt,
Es reifen die Früchte durch der Sonne Macht.

So keimet die Seele in des Herzens Schrein,
So sprosset des Menschen Geist im Licht der Welt,
So reifet des Menschen Kraft in Gottes Schein.

Und Wurzel und Blatt und der Früchtesegen,
Sie halten des Menschen Erdenleben;
Und Seele und Geïst und Kraftbewegen,
Sie mögen sich dankend zu Gott erheben.
    Amen. —

The plant roots quicken in the night of the earth,
The leaves unfold through the might of the air,
The fruits grow ripe through the power of the sun.

So quickens the soul in the shrine of the heart,
So man's spirit unfolds in the light of the world,
So ripens man's strength in the glory of God.

And root and leaf and the ripe fruit's blessing
Support the life of men on earth;
And soul and spirit and the strong deed's action
May raise themselves in gratitude to God.
      Amen. —

Das Licht macht sichtbar
Stein, Pflanze, Tier und Mensch,
Die Seele macht lebendig
Kopf, Herz, Hand und Fuss.

Es freut sich das Licht,
Wenn Steine glänzen,
Pflanzen blühen, Tiere laufen
Und Menschen Arbeit leisten.

So soll die Seele sich freuen,
Wenn das Herz — sich wärmend weitet,
Gedanken lichtvoll kraften,
Beherzter Wille wirkt.

The sun illumines
Stone, plant, beast and man.
Our soul enlivens
Head, heart, hand and foot.

The light rejoices
When stones sparkle,
Plants bloom, beasts run,
And men work.

So should our soul rejoice
When our heart grows warm and wide,
Enlightened thoughts grow strong,
Enheartened will can work.

Die Sonne gibt
Den Pflanzen Licht,
Weil die Sonne
Die Pflanzen liebt.
So gibt Seelenlicht
Ein Mensch andern Menschen,
Wenn er sie liebt.

The sun gives light
To the plants,
For the sun
Does love the plants.
So one man gives soul-light
To others
When he loves them.

FÜR EIN JÜNGERES KIND

Vom Kopf zum Fuss
Durch Herz und Hand
Bin ich Gottes Kind,
In Sonne und im Monde,
In Stern und Stein
Fühl ich Gottes Kraft,
In Vater und in Mutter,
In allen lieben Menschen
Lebt mir Gottes Wille.
So will auch ich
Als Gottes Kind
Durch Gottes Kraft,
Nach Gottes Willen
Leben und sprechen
Und, was ich soll,
Gott getreu auch tun.

FOR A YOUNGER CHILD

From head to foot,
Through heart and hand,
I am a child of God;
In sun and moon,
In star and stone,
I feel the strength of God;
In father and mother,
In all dear people
God's will is alive for me.
So will I too,
As child of God,
Through power of God,
In will of God,
Live and speak
And what I ought
Do faithfully to God.

Mit meinen Augen
Beschaue ich die Welt,
Des Gottes schöne Welt,
Und danken muss mein Herz,
Dass es leben darf
In dieser Gotteswelt,
Dass ich erwachen darf
In des Tages Helligkeit
Und des Nachts ich ruhen darf
In Gottes Seligkeit.

With my own eyes
I see the world,
The lovely world of God.
My heart must thank
That I may live
In this, God's world,
That I may wake
In the brightness of day,
And may rest in the night
In the blessing of God.

Die Sonne sendet
Zur Erde ihr Licht;
Der Gottesgeist,
Er strahlet hell
Im Sonnenlicht.
Die Pflanzen trinken
Das Sonnenlicht,
So wachsen sie
Auf Feld und Wiese
Und sind des Gottesgeistes
Geliebte Kinder —
Und Menschen tragen
Im Herzen und in der Seele
Den Gottesgeist;
In ihren Händen
Da wirket der Gottesgeist;
Ich liebe den Gottesgeist,
Weil er in mir lebet.

The sun sends forth
To earth its light;
God's spirit shines
In sunlight bright.
The plants all drink
The sunlight in,
And so they grow
On field and meadow,
Belovéd children
Of the spirit of God —
And humans bear
In heart and soul
God's spirit too;
And in their hands
God's spirit works;
I love the Spirit of God
Because He lives in me.

Die Sonne sendet
Zur Erde Licht;
Der Gottes-Geist,
Er strahlet hell
Im Sonnenlicht.
Die Pflanzen trinken
Das Sonnenlicht,
So wachsen sie
Auf Feld und Berg
Als Gottes Werk.
Und auch der Mensch,
Er trägt in Herz
Und Seele Gott.
Und seine Hände
Bewegen sich
Durch Gottesgeist.
Ich liebe ihn,
Den Gottesgeist,
In Herz und Händen,
In Sonn' und Mond.

The sun sends forth
To earth its light;
God's spirit shines
In sunlight bright.
The plants all drink
The sunlight in,
And so they grow
On field and hill
As works of God.
Man too bears God
In heart and soul,
And his hands move
Thro' spirit of God.
I love God's spirit
In heart and hands,
In sun and moon.

Oben stehet die Sonne,
Sie schenkt mir liebes Licht;
Im Lichte gibt mir Gott
Die edle Kraft des Lebens,
Und des Gottes Kraft,
Sie strahlet überall
In jedem Stein,
In allen Pflanzen,
In Tieren und Menschen —
Und wenn auch
In meinem Herzen
Die Liebe wohnen kann,
Dann ziehet Gottes Kraft
Auch in mich selbst hinein,
Die hohe Gotteskraft,
Die Christus den Menschen
Auf Erden hat geschenkt.

Es freuet sich das Menschenauge
Am Schein der leuchtenden Sonne.
So freue die Seele sich auch
Am Gottesgeiste, der in allem lebt
Als die unsichtbare Sonne,
Die jedem Wesen liebend leuchtet.

The sun stands high above,
It gives me kindly light;
In light God gives me strength,
The noble strength of life;
The strength of God
Streams everywhere
In every stone,
In all the plants,
In animals and men.
And if in my own heart
Love also finds a home,
God's strength will enter
My own Self,
The mighty strength of God
Which Christ has given
To us, mankind on earth.

The eye of man is glad
In the light cast by the shining sun.
So may our soul rejoice
In the spirit of God, who lives
In all, as sun unseen,
Casting its light in love for every being.

Ich schau' in die Sternenwelt —
Ich verstehe der Sterne Glanz,
Wenn ich in ihm schauen kann
Gottes weisheitsvolles Weltenlenken.
Ich schau' ins eigne Herz —
Ich verstehe des Herzens Schlag,
Wenn ich in ihm spüren kann
Gottes gütevolles Menschenlenken.
Ich verstehe nichts vom Sternenglanz
Und auch nichts vom Herzensschlag,
Wenn ich Gott nicht schau' und spüre.
Und Gott hat meine Seele
Geführt in dieses Leben;
Er wird sie führen zu immer neuen Leben:
So sagt, wer richtig denken kann.
Und jedes Jahr, das man weiter lebt,
Spricht mehr von Gott und Seelenewigkeit.

I look into the world of stars —
I understand their splendour
If I can behold in it
God's wisdom guiding the world.
I look into my own heart —
I understand my heart's beat,
If I can feel within it
God's goodness guiding men.
I understand nothing of the starry splendour,
And nothing of the beat of my heart,
If I see not and feel not God.
God has led my soul
Into this life,
And He will lead it to ever new life:
So say all who can rightly think.
And every further year we live,
Speaks more of God and the soul everlasting.

Wie die Sonne am Himmel
Täglich das Licht der Erde sendet,
So soll meine Seele täglich
Sich zu rechtem Tun ermahnen;
Dass ich werde ein ganzer Mensch:
Leib, Seele und Geist
Für Zeit und Ewigkeit.

As the sun in the sky
Sends light to the earth each day,
So should my soul each day
Arouse itself to rightful deeds;
That I become a human being whole:
Body, Soul and Spirit
In time and in eternity.

Der Sonne liebes Licht,
Es hellet mir den Tag;
Der Seele Geistesmacht,
Sie gibt den Gliedern Kraft;
Im Sonnen-Lichtes-Glanz
Verehre ich, O Gott,
Die Menschenkraft, die Du
In meine Seele mir
So gütig hast gepflanzt,
Dass ich kann arbeitsam
Und lernbegierig sein.
Von Dir stammt Licht und Kraft,
Zu Dir ström Lieb und Dank.

MORNING VERSE FOR THE FOUR LOWER CLASSES

The sun with loving light
Makes bright for me each day;
The soul with spirit power
Gives strength unto my limbs;
In sunlight shining clear
I reverence, O God,
The strength of humankind,
That thou so graciously
Hast planted in my soul,
That I with all my might
May love to work and learn.
From Thee come light and strength,
To Thee rise love and thanks.

MORGENSPRUCH FÜR DIE OBEREN KLASSEN

Ich schaue in die Welt;
In der die Sonne leuchtet,
In der die Sterne funkeln,
In der die Steine lagern,
Die Pflanzen lebend wachsen,
Die Tiere fühlend leben,
In der der Mensch beseelt
Dem Geiste Wohnung gibt;
Ich schaue in die Seele,
Die mir im Innern lebet.
Der Gottesgeist, er weht
Im Sonn'- und Seelenlicht,
Im Weltenraum, da draussen,
In Seelentiefen, drinnen. —
Zu Dir, O Gottesgeist,
Will bittend ich mich wenden,
Dass Kraft und Segen mir
Zum Lernen und zur Arbeit
In meinem Innern wachse.

MORNING VERSE FOR THE HIGHER CLASSES

I look into the world;
In which the sun shines,
In which the stars sparkle,
In which the stones lie,
The living plants are growing,
The animals are feeling,
In which the soul of man
Gives dwelling for the spirit;
I look into the soul
Which lives within myself.
God's spirit weaves in light
Of sun and human soul,
In world of space, without,
In depths of soul, within.
God's spirit, 'tis to Thee
I turn myself in prayer,
That strength and blessing grow
In me, to learn and work.

ABENDGLOCKENGEBET

Das Schöne bewundern,
Das Wahre behüten,
Das Edle verehren,
Das Gute beschliessen:
Es führet den Menschen
Im Leben zu Zielen,
Im Handeln zum Rechten,
Im Fühlen zum Frieden,
Im Denken zum Lichte;
Und lehrt ihn vertrauen
Auf göttliches Walten
In allem, was ist:
In Weltenall,
Im Seelengrund.

PRAYER AT THE EVENING BELL

To wonder at Beauty,
To watch over Truth,
To esteem what is noble,
To resolve on the Good:
It leads human beings
To Aims in their life,
To Right in their action,
To Peace in their feeling,
To light in their thinking;
And teaches them trust
In the working of God
In all that exists:
In all the world,
In depths of soul.

CONCERNING THE TRANSCRIPTS OF THE LECTURES

From *Rudolf Steiner, An Autobiography*, Chapter 35, 2nd edition, 1980, published by Multimedia Pub. Corp., New York.

Two consequences of my anthroposophical activity are the books which were made accessible to the general public and an extensive series of lecture courses which were initially intended for private circulation and were available only to members of the Theosophical (later Anthroposophical) Society. The transcripts of the latter were taken down — some more accurately than others — during my lectures. But time did not permit me to undertake their correction. I, for my part, would have preferred spoken word to remain spoken word, but the Members were in favour of private publication of the Courses. And so it came about. If I had had time to correct the transcripts, the reservation "For Members Only" need not have been made from the very first. Now it has been dropped for over a year.

Here in my Autobiography it is above all necessary to explain how the two — the publications in general and in private circulation — are accommodated in my elaboration of Anthroposophy.

Whoever wishes to pursue my own inner conflict and toil in my effort to introduce Anthroposophy to contemporary thought, must do so with the aid of the works in general circulation which include analysis of all forms of cognition of this age. Therein also lies that which crystallised within me in "spiritual vision" and from which came into existence the structure of Anthroposophy, even if imperfect in many respects.

Apart from this obligation to construct Anthroposophy and thereby to serve only that which ensues when communications from the Spirit World are to be transmitted to modern civilisation, the need also arose to meet the claims which were manifested within the Membership as a compulsion, a yearning of the soul.

Above all, many Members were greatly disposed to hearing the Gospels and the scriptural content of the Bible presented in an anthroposophical light. Courses were requested which were to examine such revelations to humanity.

Internal courses were held to meet this requirement. At these lectures only Members were present who were initiated in Anthroposophy. It was possible to speak to them as to those well-versed in Anthroposophy. The delivery of these internal lectures was such as simply could not be communicated in written works intended for the general public.

In these closed circles I was able to discuss subjects which I would have had to present quite differently if they had been intended for a general public from the very first.

Thus in the duality of the public and private works there actually exists something of two-fold diverse origin. The wholly public writings are a result of that which struggled and toiled within me; in the private publications, the Society struggles and toils with me. I listen to the vibrations within the soul-life of the Membership and within my own being and the tone of the lectures arises from what I hear there.

Nowhere has even the slightest mention of anything been made which does not proceed from the substance of Anthroposophy. No concessions can be made to any prejudices or presentiments existing within the Membership. Whoever reads these private publications can accept them as a true representation of anthroposophical conviction. Thus when petitions became more urgent, the ruling as to the private circulation of these publications within the Membership could be amended without any hesitation. Any errors occurring in transcripts which I have not been able to revise will however have to be tolerated.

The right to pass judgment on the content of any such private publication is nevertheless reserved to those possessing the prerequisite to do so. For the great majority of these publications, this is *at least* an anthroposophical knowledge of man and the universe, in so far as its essence is presented in Anthroposophy, and of "the history of anthroposophy" such as it is derived from communications from the Spirit-World.

Complete Edition of the works of Rudolf Steiner in German, published by the Rudolf Steiner Verlag, Dornach, Switzerland, by whom all rights are reserved.

Writings

1. Works written between 1883 and 1925
2. Essays and articles written between 1882 and 1925
3. Letters, drafts, manuscripts, fragments, verses, inscriptions, meditative sayings, etc.

Lectures

1. Public Lectures
2. Lectures to Members of the Anthroposophical Society on general anthroposophical subjects.
   Lectures to Members on the history of the Anthroposophical Movement and Anthroposophical Society
3. Lectures and Courses on special branches of work:
   Art: Eurythmy, Speech and Drama, Music, Visual Arts, History of Art
   Education
   Medicine and Therapy
   Science
   Sociology and the Threefold Social Order
   Lectures given to Workmen at the Goetheanum

The total number of lectures amount to some six thousand, shorthand reports of which are available in the case of the great majority.

Reproductions and Sketches

Paintings in water colour, drawings, coloured diagrams, Eurythmy forms, etc.

When the Edition is complete the total number of volumes, each of a considerable size, will amount to several hundreds. A full and detailed Bibliographical Survey, with subjects, dates and places where the lectures were given is available. All the volumes can be obtained from the Rudolf Steiner Press in London as well as directly from the Rudolf Steiner Verlag, Dornach, Switzerland.

71